GETTING TO KNOW
THE U.S. PRESIDENTS

A B R A H A M
LINCOLN

SIXTEENTH PRESIDENT
1861 – 1865

WRITTEN AND ILLUSTRATED BY MIKE VENEZIA

CHILDREN'S PRESS®
A DIVISION OF SCHOLASTIC INC.
NEW YORK   TORONTO   LONDON   AUCKLAND   SYDNEY
MEXICO CITY   NEW DELHI   HONG KONG
DANBURY, CONNECTICUT

Reading Consultant: Nanci R. Vargus, Ed.D., Assistant Professor, School of Education, University of Indianapolis

Historical Consultant: Marc J. Selverstone, Ph.D., Assistant Professor, Miller Center of Public Affairs, University of Virginia

Photographs © 2005: Art Resource, NY: 25 (Museum of the City of New York, NY/Scala), 8 (SEF); Bridgeman Art Library International Ltd., London/New York: 29 (Jean Leon Jerome Ferris/Private Collection), 21 (Friedrich Schultz/Hirshhorn Museum, Washington, DC. U.S.A.); City of Springfield Convention and Visitors Bureau: 14; Corbis Images: 12, 22, 24, 28 (Bettmann), 3 (Mathew B. Brady), 23 (Mathew B. Brady/Bettmann), 26 (John Adams Elder/The Corcoran Gallery of Art); Getty Images/MPI/Hulton Archive: 30; Library of Congress: 32 (Alexander Gardner), 6, 10, 20; North Wind Picture Archives: 13; PictureHistory.com: 16; Superstock, Inc.: 19.

Colorist for illustrations: Dave Ludwig

Library of Congress Cataloging-in-Publication Data

Venezia, Mike.
    Abraham Lincoln / written and illustrated by Mike Venezia.
        p. cm. — (Getting to know the U.S. presidents)
    ISBN 0-516-22621-5 (lib. bdg.)   0-516-25483-9 (pbk.)
    1. Lincoln, Abraham, 1809-1865—Juvenile literature. 2.
Presidents-—United States—Biography—Juvenile literature. I. Title.
    E457.905.V46 2005
    973.7'092–dc22

                                        2004022573

    6 7 8 9 10 R 14 13 12 11 10   08

An 1864 photograph of President Lincoln by Mathew Brady

Abraham Lincoln was born in a small, dirt-floor log cabin in Harden County, Kentucky, in 1809. As the sixteenth president, Abraham Lincoln guided the United States through its most difficult period ever. Because of Lincoln's strong leadership and wise decisions, many historians call him the greatest of all American presidents.

By the time Abraham Lincoln started his job as president, the United States had reached the boiling point over what to do about slavery. Most southerners felt that owning slaves was their legal right, and that slavery should be allowed to spread into new territories and states. Many northerners felt slavery was very wrong and should be stopped right away.

Finally, after years of trying to work things

out, southern states decided they would be better off breaking away, or seceding from, the United States. In 1861, they formed their own country and called it the Confederate States of America. It didn't take long before disagreements between the North and South led to a terrible war.

The Civil War was the major event of Abraham Lincoln's presidency.

People in the South always had the idea that each state in the Union was almost like a separate little country. They believed that they could leave the United States if there was a good reason. People from the northern states, including Abraham Lincoln, believed the United States was a permanent country and that all the states had to stick together to make it work.

Abe Lincoln spent most of his time as president doing everything he could to get the United States back together. It was an extremely difficult job. By the time the Civil War ended, almost 620,000 soldiers had died. That's as many Americans as died in almost all other American wars combined. This includes the American Revolution, the War of 1812, the Spanish-American War, World War I, World War II, and the wars in Korea and Vietnam.

When Abe Lincoln was growing up, no one would have ever guessed he would become president of the United States someday. Abe's father was a poor farmer. He moved his family from the wilderness areas of Kentucky to Indiana and then to Illinois, always hoping to find better farmland.

A replica of Lincoln's boyhood home in Kentucky

As soon as Abe could hold an ax, his father put him to work chopping down trees, clearing land, and helping build log cabins. Abe and his sister Sarah had only a few months of schooling while they were growing up. A teacher in a backwoods area was usually just anyone who came along who could read or write. It wasn't the best way to learn, but Abe got an idea of how to read, write, and do arithmetic.

Even as a boy,
Abe Lincoln loved
to read.

When Abe was nine years old, his mother died. Abe missed her very much but cheered up a little when his father remarried a year later. Abe got along great with his new stepmother, Sarah Johnston Lincoln. Sarah encouraged Abe to read. He didn't need much encouragement, though. Abe found he loved to read more than just about anything!

It seemed as if Abraham Lincoln always had a borrowed book in his hand. Abe would even read while he was plowing fields. Some of his favorite books were *Robinson Crusoe*, *Aesop's Fables*, the Bible, a book about George Washington, and especially, the plays and poems of William Shakespeare.

This painting shows Abraham Lincoln splitting rails as a young man.

Abraham Lincoln was a tall, super-skinny boy. He amazed people, though, with his strength and energy. He could chop down more trees and split rails faster than most grown men.

Even though he was good at farming, Abe never really liked it that much. Reading books had fired up his imagination. Abe knew there was an exciting world outside the wilderness, and he wanted to be a part of it.

Lincoln worked for a while on a flatboat like this one.

At the age of twenty-two, Abe left home and started trying different jobs. He delivered goods down the Mississippi River to New Orleans on a flatboat, and worked on a large riverboat. Before he became president, Abe was also a soldier in the Black Hawk War, a surveyor, a postmaster, a store owner, a lawyer, and an Illinois state representative!

New Salem, Illinois, has been restored to look the way it did when Lincoln lived there.

One of Abraham Lincoln's first jobs was managing a general store in the small town of New Salem, Illinois. The store became a meeting place for townspeople. Abe loved discussing the latest news and events of the day. He made many new friends at the store.

People in New Salem enjoyed Abe's company. He was a great storyteller and told the best jokes around. Everyone was impressed with Abe's strength, too. Once, some townspeople set up a wrestling match between Abe and the town bully. Abe easily won the contest. New Salem was a rough-and-tumble town and Abe Lincoln fit in just fine.

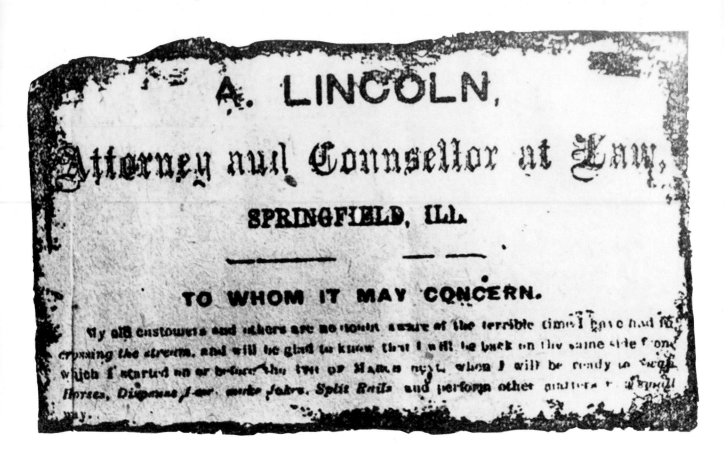

A business card Lincoln used when he was a young lawyer

When Abe Lincoln moved to New Salem, he was old enough to vote. He soon became interested in how his state's government worked. Abe enjoyed politics a lot and thought he would run for the Illinois State Legislature. Abe lost his first election, but tried again a few years later and won. People in the area really liked Abe's friendly, honest style.

While he was serving as a state representative, Abe decided to become a lawyer. He never went to law school, though. Abraham Lincoln learned everything he needed by reading books. People would often see Abe lying under a tree reading to himself. He would argue both sides of a court case out loud until he understood how the law worked. Abe passed his law exam in 1836.

Abraham Lincoln served four terms as a
legislator, coming up with new ideas and laws
to help improve his state. During this time he
met and fell in love with a girl named Mary
Todd. Abe always felt awkward around girls.
By now he was 6 feet, 4 inches tall and still
very skinny. Mary, on the other hand, was a
little bit plump and only 5 feet tall.

A portrait of the Lincoln family during Lincoln's presidency

Abe and Mary didn't care about looks, though. They were crazy about each other and decided to get married. Unfortunately, over the years, Abe and Mary's marriage became filled with sadness. Only one of their four sons lived to be an adult. As parents, Abe and Mary went through many long periods of depression.

A photograph of Abraham Lincoln in 1846, when he was elected to the U.S. House of Representatives

In 1846, Abraham Lincoln was elected to the U.S. House of Representatives. During this time, he suggested a law that would end slavery in the nation's capital, the District of Columbia. Abe had seen a slave market for the first time when he traveled to New Orleans as a young man. The idea of buying and selling human beings bothered him for the rest of his life.

The Slave Market, by Friedrich Schulz (Hirshhorn Museum, Washington, D.C.)

Abe's law wasn't accepted, but he started getting attention as someone who might be able to do something about solving the nation's slavery problem. Abe really got attention, though, when he decided to run for the U.S. Senate in 1858.

Abraham Lincoln speaking during the 1858 Lincoln-Douglas Debates

Abe could see that recent laws and decisions were making it easier for slavery to spread into new territories. This was exactly the opposite of what Abe Lincoln hoped would happen. He thought if he became a U.S. senator, he might be able to do more to prevent slavery from spreading.

Abe ran against a popular politician named Stephen A. Douglas. Abe challenged Stephen Douglas to a series of debates. A debate is a contest in which people point out why their ideas are better than the other person's. Stephen Douglas argued that new territories

should have the right to decide for themselves whether or not to allow slavery. Abe Lincoln argued that slavery was just plain wrong and should never spread into new territories or states.

A photograph of Stephen Douglas

This photograph shows Lincoln the summer before he was elected president. That fall, a little girl wrote him a letter saying he would look better if he grew a beard. Lincoln took her advice. By the time of his inauguration, he had grown his famous beard.

Even though Stephen Douglas won the election for senator, people all over the country learned about Abraham Lincoln during the exciting debates. Many Americans were impressed with Lincoln's intelligence, sense of humor, honesty, and powerful speeches. In 1860, Abraham Lincoln was chosen by the Republican Party to run for president.

The Civil War began when Confederate troops attacked Fort Sumter on April 12, 1861.

Abe won the election. When he took office in 1861, the United States was on the brink of civil war. On April 12 of that year, Confederate soldiers fired their cannons on Fort Sumter in South Carolina. This attack on a U.S. government fort became the start of the Civil War.

A portrait of T. J. "Stonewall" Jackson by John Adams (The Corcoran Gallery of Art)

When the war began, President Lincoln didn't think it would last very long. Most people agreed with him. Lincoln hoped that after the Confederate states thought it over for a while, they would change their minds and rejoin the United States. People in the North were so sure they would soon win that they showed up to watch the first big battle of the war at Bull Run in the state of Virginia.

People brought picnic baskets and expected to see something like a sports event. Things didn't work out that way, though. A southern general who became known as "Stonewall" Jackson and his men beat the northern troops badly. Before they knew what was happening, the picnickers were interrupted by soldiers running for their lives.

President Lincoln visits Union troops after the bloody Battle of Antietam in 1862.

The northern states had more soldiers, more factories to make ammunition, and more money to run a war. But the Confederate states had something the North didn't have— a bunch of great generals. Southern armies led by General Robert E. Lee won many early battles of the Civil War.

It took three years of fighting before President Lincoln finally found a general who could beat the Confederate army. Ulysses S. Grant was a tough, no-nonsense soldier who finally led the northern states to victory.

A painting showing Confederate general Robert E. Lee (right) surrendering to Union general Ulysses S. Grant (left)

An illustration showing President Lincoln working on the Emancipation Proclamation

When the Civil War began, President Lincoln said it was a fight to keep the United States together as one country. As the war went on, though, he changed his mind. Abraham Lincoln realized the war was really about slavery and it wasn't going to end until slavery was stopped. On January 1, 1863, President Lincoln sent out the Emancipation Proclamation. This announcement was an order to free all slaves in states that were rebelling against the Union. Slave owners in the South weren't about to obey their enemy's demand, though.

The Emancipation Proclamation did, however, make it clear why the Civil War was being fought. It later led to the Thirteenth Amendment. This amendment, which was added to the Constitution a few months after Lincoln died, finally did end slavery throughout the entire United States.

On April 9, 1865, soon after Abraham Lincoln was elected for a second term as president, the Civil War finally ended. After more than four years of bloody fighting, a worn-out President Lincoln prepared to welcome the southern states back into the Union.

This is one of the last photographs taken of Abraham Lincoln. His face shows the strain of four difficult, war-torn years.

Five days after the Civil War ended, Abe and Mary went to see a play and relax. During the play, a hate-filled southern actor named John Wilkes Booth shot President Lincoln. The next morning, on April 15, 1865, the president who had led his nation through its worst time in history died. People across the country were shocked and saddened.

In 1863, during the worst part of the war, Lincoln had given an amazing speech that became known as the Gettysburg Address. He reminded Americans that the United States was a special nation "conceived in liberty and dedicated to the proposition that all men are created equal." Today, people still love and remember Abraham Lincoln because he worked so hard to make sure the United States lived up to these ideals.